I0050564

UZBEKISTAN'S ECOSYSTEM FOR TECHNOLOGY STARTUPS

Dilshod Zufarov, Aimee Hampel-Milagrosa,
Vishal Aditya Potluri, and Paul Vandenberg

AUGUST 2023

Country Report No. 9
Ecosystems for Technology Startups in Asia and the Pacific

ASIAN DEVELOPMENT BANK

ADB

Creative Commons Attribution 3.0 IGO license (CC BY 3.0 IGO)

© 2023 Asian Development Bank
6 ADB Avenue, Mandaluyong City, 1550 Metro Manila, Philippines
Tel +63 2 8632 4444; Fax +63 2 8636 2444
www.adb.org

Some rights reserved. Published in 2023.

ISBN 978-92-9270-250-2 (print); 978-92-9270-251-9 (electronic); 978-92-9270-252-6 (ebook)
Publication Stock No. TCS230277-2
DOI: http://dx.doi.org/10.22617/TCS230277-2

The views expressed in this publication are those of the authors and do not necessarily reflect the views and policies of the Asian Development Bank (ADB) or its Board of Governors or the governments they represent.

ADB does not guarantee the accuracy of the data included in this publication and accepts no responsibility for any consequence of their use. The mention of specific companies or products of manufacturers does not imply that they are endorsed or recommended by ADB in preference to others of a similar nature that are not mentioned.

By making any designation of or reference to a particular territory or geographic area, or by using the term "country" in this publication, ADB does not intend to make any judgments as to the legal or other status of any territory or area.

This publication is available under the Creative Commons Attribution 3.0 IGO license (CC BY 3.0 IGO) https://creativecommons.org/licenses/by/3.0/igo/. By using the content of this publication, you agree to be bound by the terms of this license. For attribution, translations, adaptations, and permissions, please read the provisions and terms of use at https://www.adb.org/terms-use#openaccess.

This CC license does not apply to non-ADB copyright materials in this publication. If the material is attributed to another source, please contact the copyright owner or publisher of that source for permission to reproduce it. ADB cannot be held liable for any claims that arise as a result of your use of the material.

Please contact pubsmarketing@adb.org if you have questions or comments with respect to content, or if you wish to obtain copyright permission for your intended use that does not fall within these terms, or for permission to use the ADB logo.

Corrigenda to ADB publications may be found at http://www.adb.org/publications/corrigenda.

Note:
In this publication, "$" refers to United States dollars.

All photos are owned by ADB unless otherwise stated.

Cover design by Joe Mark Ganaban.

Contents

Tables and Boxes

Foreword

New digital technologies and their innovative use in the provision of goods and services are a major disruptor in the business world in Uzbekistan and other countries. Today, we can use digital methods to order food, hail a taxi, move money, arrange travel, watch entertainment, and shop for just about anything. At a deeper and often less visible level, technology is affecting production processes in the form of Industry 4.0. Technology-based startup enterprises—or tech startups, for short—are an important part of the evolving business-to-business and business-to-consumer landscape in Central Asia as well as globally.

Uzbekistan startups develop in an ecosystem that can support—or hinder—their development. That ecosystem involves many national elements, but regional and international factors also are important, especially as the economy becomes increasingly open and globalized. Access to finance and skilled personnel, including both tech experts and entrepreneurs, are important parts of the ecosystem. Good digital infrastructure and supportive government policy are also critical. Startups develop best when the markets for their goods and services are large and active.

This report analyzes Uzbekistan's ecosystem and assesses the extent to which it is supportive of the growing number of startups. The report focuses on startups in four areas: healthtech, agritech, edtech, and cleantech. These four areas not only contribute to economic activity but can have a deeper impact on socioeconomic development. Edtech and healthtech contribute to human capital formation while agritech improves productivity and raises incomes in the rural sector where many of the poor people work. Greentech advances environmental sustainability and climate change mitigation.

This analysis of the startup ecosystem provides recommendations for policy makers in Uzbekistan and other countries in Central Asia. Our hope is that improved ecosystems can better support startups throughout the Asia and Pacific region.

Albert Park
Chief Economist and Director General
Economic Research and Development Impact Department
Asian Development Bank

Yevgeniy Zhukov
Director General
Central and West Asia Department
Asian Development Bank

Acknowledgments

The report was prepared by Dilshod Zufarov, consultant, with contributions from Vishal Aditya Potluri, Aimee Hampel-Milagrosa, and Paul Vandenberg of the Asian Development Bank (ADB). Saad Paracha, Rana Hasan, and Lei Lei Song provided management support.

ADB's Uzbekistan Resident Mission reviewed the report and facilitated interaction with the Government of Uzbekistan. The authors would like to thank key experts from government, incubators, accelerators, development partners, investors, academic institutions, and startups who provided invaluable insights to the researchers. The draft report was reviewed by the Ministry of Digital Technologies of the Republic of Uzbekistan.

Tuesday Soriano copyedited the report. Amanda Isabel Mamon and Muhammad Muddassir Naveed provided administrative support, contracting, and manuscript management.

Abbreviations

AID	Agency for Innovative Development
COVID-19	coronavirus disease
ICT	information and communication technology
MDITC	Ministry for Development of Information Technologies and Communications
MID	Ministry of Innovative Development

Executive Summary

Reforms since the mid-2010s have prioritized private sector development and opened Uzbekistan's economy to the world. Efforts are being made to diversify away from heavy reliance on natural resources and commodity exports. As part of these efforts, the government has encouraged innovation and entrepreneurship. It has recognized the important role of technology-based startup enterprises (tech startups) and introduced a range of policies, structures, and programs to support them.

Government policies and programs are part of the wider startup ecosystem, which includes financiers, private incubators and accelerators, and talent (human capital). The ecosystem in Uzbekistan is deepening, but still has substantial room for development—in the quality of support it provides, the type of support it offers, and the number of startups it reaches. The startup community itself is at a nascent stage of development, with a very high number of startups in the pre-seed and seed stages. More entrepreneurs need to come forward to turn innovative ideas into viable business models, and more existing startups need to grow to scale.

This report examines the nature of startups and the ecosystem in Uzbekistan. It highlights the strengths and weaknesses of the ecosystem and identifies the current opportunities and challenges for startups. It aims to improve our understanding of the startup community and provides recommendations to further improve the system.

The report focuses on startups in four market segments: health (healthtech), agriculture (agritech), education (edtech), and environment and climate change (cleantech, also known as greentech). These segments were chosen because startups not only contribute to economic activity but can also have an important impact on human development. Healthtech and edtech support human capital development. Agritech can help raise the income of farmers and low-income households in rural areas. Cleantech can help society mitigate and adapt to climate change. These segments are small but growing. Two other segments—fintech and e-commerce, including e-marketplace—make up the largest part of the startup community.

It is difficult to determine the number of startups currently operating in the country. According to our estimate, there were almost 1,200 in 2020 and there will be more by 2023. Most of them are at a very early stage of development (i.e., pre-seed and also seed stage). At these stages, products are still being designed and refined, and many are not yet on the market or have only recently been launched.

For this study, 31 startups in the four sectors were surveyed and interviewed. While the sample is not fully representative, it does offer insights into the nature of the startup community. As expected, startups are heavily concentrated in the capital city of Tashkent (three-quarters of respondents). About one quarter were founded by women, and the average age of founders was 31. Most founders have a bachelor's degree, and a few have a doctorate.

The personal, business, and economic impact of the coronavirus disease (COVID-19) pandemic was significant. Many sectors suffered losses, but the pandemic also increased demand for digital services offered by startups. In particular, it created new opportunities in edtech and healthtech. In the longer term, Uzbekistan's young and growing population, combined with increases in school enrollment, will provide a large market for edtech.

Agriculture is an important sector, employing half of the workforce and generating over one-fifth of economic output. Agritech innovations can help increase productivity and output and better connect farmers to markets. Since many facets of the sector are still controlled or influenced by the government, it is important for the government to be an adopter and a promoter of innovation among farmers through extension services, awareness building, and training.

Lack of external funding is a critical constraint for startups. Initial financing comes from the founders' own resources (e.g., savings, salary) and contributions from family and friends. This is a common approach in other countries. However, additional funding is needed, especially in the pre-seed and seed stages, for product development, staffing, and business formation. Government grants are helpful in this regard. However, angel investment and venture capital are still scarce and need to be developed. The National Venture Fund is set up, and some corporate venture capital is emerging. A legal and regulatory framework for private venture capital is needed to encourage this form of financing.

Several incubators and accelerators have been established to provide training, guidance, and advice to young startups. The quality of these programs can be improved, especially by ensuring that managers and trainers have real-world business knowledge and experience. Programs should provide (or provide links to) experienced mentors. However, the number of mentors is low, and efforts could be made to establish a better cadre through training and incentives (payment) for their mentoring services.

Talent, both entrepreneurial and technological, is a critical component of the ecosystem. Good talent is available, but in some areas, it is in short supply, especially among developers and programmers. Some universities offer entrepreneurship training, but more lecturers with real business experience are needed to make it more relevant. The startups we surveyed generally did not see high staff turnover as a problem.

Government has enormous spending power and can be an important market for startups. This is true not only for ministries, but also for schools in edtech and hospitals in healthtech. However, government agencies are generally reluctant to procure from startups and instead develop their own solutions in-house or source them from foreign vendors. A startup-friendly approach and clear procurement and collaboration policies would change the culture and provide incentives to source from small, young firms.

The Ministry of Higher Education, Science and Innovation and the Ministry of Digital Technologies provide the necessary sector-specific support for startups. To promote holistic development, more attention could be paid to ecosystem-wide strategy and coordination.

Introduction

Since 2016, Uzbekistan has implemented a number of important economic reforms. The country has sought to reduce its heavy reliance on raw material exports, particularly natural gas, gold, cotton, and copper. Prices for these exports can fluctuate significantly, causing domestic instability. The government sought to build a more stable economic base through economic diversification and private sector development.

The government approved the Action Strategy 2017–2021, based on an analysis of entrepreneurship, existing regulations, and other countries' strategies (Government of Uzbekistan 2017). Reforms were implemented in a number of areas, including banking, taxation, trade, and privatization of state-owned enterprises. As a result, the economy has become more open and market-oriented.

The reforms took place at a time when the role of innovation and technology—particularly digital technology—in economic development was increasingly recognized worldwide. This period saw the emergence of a new type of business organization: technology-based startup enterprises, or tech startups.

The government has sought to foster the twin activities of technological innovation and entrepreneurship, including the role of tech startups. It created the Ministry for Development of Information Technologies and Communications (MDITC) in 2015 and the Ministry of Innovative Development (MID) 2 years later.[1] 2018 was declared the Year of Support for Active Entrepreneurship, Innovative Ideas, and Technologies. New policies and programs were developed to support innovation and tech startups. These measures have helped to start the process of building a quality ecosystem for tech startups.

Against this background, this study provides an analysis of Uzbekistan's startup ecosystem, including the startups themselves. The report highlights the strengths and weaknesses of the ecosystem and offers insights directly from startups on how

---

[1] MDITC was created in 2015 out of a preexisting government unit. In early 2023, MID became the Agency for Innovative Development and is under the Ministry of Higher Education, Science and Innovation.

they view the support offered and the gaps and challenges that remain. The final section provides recommendations for the government and other stakeholders to further improve the system.

1.1   Defining Tech Startups and the Ecosystem

Tech startups are young enterprises that have devised an innovative technology or are using an existing technology to structure a unique business model (Durban 2021). Most startups are considered highly scalable, meaning they can expand rapidly, because they are often internet-based and can therefore quickly replicate their services and attract thousands or millions of customers. The potential for rapid growth is therefore a key characteristic of a startup.

The ecosystem is the environment in which they set up and operate. It consists of government policies, regulations, and support programs, as well as providers of finance, including but not limited to venture capital. The ecosystem also consists of incubator and accelerator programs that provide guidance, and mentors who offer advice and guidance. In addition to direct support organizations, the ecosystem also includes other business entities such as suppliers and buyers, the latter of which may be business, government, or individuals. The ecosystem also includes digital infrastructure and levels of digital and internet literacy. The culture of entrepreneurship is also a factor.

In this report, we focus on four key aspects of the ecosystem

1.   Government policies and programs
   - Facilitating laws and regulations
   - Support programs
   - Procurement opportunities

2.   Finance
   - Venture capital
   - Business angels
   - Grants, and others

3.   Incubators and accelerators
   - Associated mentors

4.   Talent
   - Schools and universities
   - Entrepreneurship and technology training programs
   - Mentoring
   - Others

It is important to recognize that startups move through several stages of development. Each stage presents unique challenges and requires specific types of support. Different experts offer different names for these stages (and their number), but the following is a common approach:

1. **Seed stage:** This is about forming an idea, developing the product, defining the mission and strategy, and finding a business model. The startup in this stage is often self-funded by the founder(s) and may be supported by funds from family and friends. Angel investment and government grants can also be used.

2. **Development stage:** This stage includes building a team, developing a minimum viable product, and market validation. Funding in this stage can come from business angels and seed venture capital.

3. **Scaling stage:** In this stage, startups seek to develop increasing traction in the target market. Funding from venture capital and private equity funds is required in this stage. As the startup generates revenue and has assets (as collateral), it can also seek a bank loan.

1.2 Methodology

To obtain a holistic picture of the ecosystem, the authors collected and analyzed information from a variety of sources. These included interviews with officials from 25 government agencies, as well as a review of industry studies, government and nongovernment websites, and other sources, including statistics and policies, laws, and regulations. An important source of information was a survey of 31 startups conducted specifically for this report. These various sources were combined to develop an understanding of the ecosystem and, most importantly, to identify its strengths and weaknesses.

This study focuses on startups in four areas: healthtech, agritech, edtech, and cleantech. These areas were selected for their potential to contribute not only to economic activity but also to human and social development. Healthtech startups can improve the health of the population. Edtech innovations can improve access to education and increase educational attainment. Agritech is important to help raise the income of poor farmers and households in rural areas. Agritech can help raise productivity and output, thereby increasing farmers' income. Cleantech startups help improve the environment and support climate change mitigation and adaptation.

Startups and the Key Components of the Ecosystem

2

The startup community in Uzbekistan is developing but is still in its infancy. Most startups have not yet moved beyond the early stages, and only a small percentage have reached the point of scaling. The ecosystem is also evolving, but needs time to grow and improve the quality of support it provides to startups. In particular, startups need better access to funding.

2.1   Number and Type of Startups

It is difficult to determine the number of startups in Uzbekistan because many of them are at a very early stage of development—formulating an idea, designing a product, and testing a prototype (Box 1). Many of them are not yet registered as enterprises. One estimate for 2020 puts the number at nearly 1,200 (Table 1). Most startups are in the seed stage and have not yet created a minimum viable

Box 1: Data on Startups and the Ecosystem

Uzbekistan lacks a systematic mechanism for collecting data on startups and the ecosystem. The existing reporting form for small and medium-sized enterprises covers all types of businesses without differentiating between those that are technology-based and non-technology-based, or between startups and traditional businesses.

In early 2020, in line with the Roadmap for Implementation of the Digital Uzbekistan, 2030 Strategy, a draft law "On Startups" was drafted. Its main purpose is to regulate and coordinate support for startups. It clarifies the concepts of startups and defines the principles and direction of support, including regulating the processes of creating startups, developing the ecosystem, and implementing preferential programs. It is the first legal document in the country to provide a precise definition of the term "startup." It also outlines the sources of funding for startups and the programs to be implemented. The draft law is expected to be submitted to the Legislative Chamber in mid-2023. It would help provide the definitions needed to accurately count startups.

In addition, it would be useful to have a single platform that provides information about startups, incubators, accelerators, mentors, foundations, business angels, and others. This information could be used to show the qualitative and quantitative progress of the ecosystem and specific sectors, as well as the dynamics of change in the support provided.

Source: Authors.

Table 1: Number of Startups by Stage, 2020

Stage	Number of Startups	Share of Total (%)	Annual Increase
Seed	1,000	85	+200
Development	150	13	+ 30
Scaling	20	2	+2
Total	1,170	100	+232

Note: The seed stage includes what are often considered pre-seed startups.
Source: Authors' estimate.

product.[2] Another 13% of startups are in the development stage, have a minimum viable product, and are generating revenue from sales. The remaining 2% are in the scaling stage. The increase in the number of startups can be attributed in part to new government initiatives and reforms, including tax incentives to support information technology (IT) startups.[3]

The Ministry of Innovative Development financed 122 startups in 2019–2022, all of which were in the development stage. A total of SUM94 billion was provided, which contributed to the creation of an estimated 1,135 jobs. Broken down by sector, 32 startups are in agriculture, 25 in ICT, 13 in energy and transport, and the rest in other sectors.

In terms of the sector as a whole, more than half of the startups are in fintech, e-commerce, and e-marketplace (Table 2). This is similar to other countries where these three sectors dominate among startups. They are followed by startups in healthtech, edtech, and enterprise resource planning.

Table 2: Startups by Sector

Sector	Sector Share (%)
Fintech	30
E-commerce (and marketplace)	27
Healthtech (medtech)	24
Edtech	18
Enterprise resource planning	15
Others	15

medtech = medical technology.
Note: Some startups are classified under more than one sector and thus the total does not sum to 100.
Source: Authors.

[2] We follow the categorization outlined in the previous chapter: seed, development, and scaling. The seed stage would include the "pre-seed" stage used in other classifications.
[3] IT Park.

The large number of fintech startups is due to the fact that 32 banks and many payment institutions in the country are developing new services that create favorable conditions for complementary activities offered by startups. Furthermore, the government passed the Law on Payments and Payment Systems in 2019 and created rules for the Issuance and Circulation of Electronic Money in 2020. This regulatory framework has created the opportunity for innovative services to emerge. Startups can apply for approval to operate as part of the electronic money system and offer services that allow customers to make digital payments.

The lower share of startups in other sectors is due to lower customer interest in tech solutions, including the government's reluctance to collaborate with and purchase from startups. Many consumers prefer to buy from traditional and established businesses. In addition, government agencies often develop their own tech solutions in-house or buy licenses from international brands rather than take the risk of working with young and unproven domestic startups.

Startup founders in Uzbekistan are young, with the average age ranging from 18 to 22, according to one source.[4] The average age of founders in our survey of startups was in the low 30s. A quarter of the startups financed by MID were led by people under 30. In comparison, founders of successful startups in developed countries are typically 35–40 years old and have more industry experience. While the situation in Uzbekistan may indicate that there is a booming startup community that attracts many young people, on the other hand, they do not have much business or sector experience, so their ventures may be less likely to succeed. About 20% of the startups financed by MID were led by women.

This age profile has two implications for startup support. First, young entrepreneurs need good business advice from incubators and mentors to compensate for the lack of experience. Second, incubation and mentoring programs should also be open to older adults to encourage them to start new ventures. Most programs currently focus on young people.

---

[4]   Uzbekistan Venture Capital Association (in Russian).

2.2 Government Strategies, Laws, and Related Measures

Since 2015, the government has been active in issuing declarations, developing strategies, and enacting laws to support innovation and entrepreneurship. Many of these measures support a better ecosystem for startups. Their impact, so far, has been difficult to determine.

To emphasize the importance of innovation, the government declared 2018 the Year of Support for Active Entrepreneurship, Innovative Ideas and Technologies. In the same year, the Innovative Development Strategy for 2019–2021 was adopted. The main objective of the strategy was to promote human capital as a key factor in fostering innovation and global competitiveness. The strategy aimed to improve the quality of education, expand its coverage to the entire population, and increase public and private investment in innovation. Toward the end of the year, a presidential decree on Improving the Mechanisms for Financing Projects in the Field of Entrepreneurship and Innovation was issued (Government of Uzbekistan 2018).

Further measures were taken in subsequent years. The Resolution of the Cabinet of Ministers on the Activities of Investment and Management Companies was adopted in May 2019. The Law on Innovation Activity was enacted in 2020 (Government of Uzbekistan 2019, 2020). Two other laws were drafted and under discussion by the end of 2022.[5] A draft law On Limited Partnerships would allow management companies (called "general partners") to manage funds of investors (called "limited partners"), which would form the basis for venture capital and related funds. In addition, a draft law On Startups would provide for government measures to encourage the private sector to invest in startups by providing financial leverage. The enactment of these two laws will encourage the development of venture capital funds and domestic financing for startups. Currently, some startups seek and receive funding in other countries where the legal structure for venture capital investment is more developed.

In July 2022, the Innovative Development Strategy 2022-2026, was approved to carry on and expand the work of the preceding strategy (see above).[6] The strategy will seek to provide support in six key areas. First, funding of SUM75 billion will be provided to 122 startup projects, which are expected to create 1,413 jobs. Second, startups will be supported to locate in technology parks and special economic zones, and the private sector will be encouraged to increase its interest in and cofinance scientific development. Third, a network of innovative infrastructure

---

[5] Regulation.gov.uz. Portal for Discussing Draft Regulatory Legal Acts. Draft Law on Limited Partnerships; and Draft Law on Startups.

[6] Resolution of the President of the Republic of Uzbekistan, July 2022, No. PF-165 "On Approval of the Innovative Development Strategy of the Republic of Uzbekistan for 2022-2026."

projects will be implemented, including innovative technological parks, technology transfer centers, innovation clusters, venture organizations, innovation centers, and incubators and accelerators. Fourth, support will be provided to encourage innovation, including acceleration, logistics, financing services, market introduction, and widening the activities of technology transfer centers. Fifth, efforts will be made to encourage the development of modern financing mechanisms for startups (such as venture capital and crowdfunding), and the expansion of simplified financing activities in a competitive environment (such as "future scientist," hackathons, and technoway marathons). And sixth, tax and customs benefits will be provided along with procedures for admission of residency in innovative technology parks and free economic zones.

2.3 Government Structures and Programs

In addition to new laws and strategies, the government has also created new structures and programs to promote innovation and technological progress. Some of these are specifically designed to support tech startups. In addition to the support programs, the government has constructed 19 innovation-related infrastructure sites, including technology parks, business incubators and accelerators, coworking centers, and others.

The Ministry for Development of Information Technologies and Communications (MDITC) was established in 2015, as part of government administrative reforms. It set up the IT Park for enterprises producing software and information technologies in 2019. Through the park and other activities, MDITC aims to (i) create favorable conditions for the development of the information technology (IT) sector; (ii) provide tenants with necessary infrastructure and consulting services; (iii) support startups through incubation and acceleration programs; and (iv) organize training in IT.

By the end of 2022, MDITC had established more than 150 IT centers across the country and trained 40,000 students in digital skills. It also supported the establishment of 450 IT companies through tax and customs incentives. It also trained more than 100 startups through incubation and acceleration programs. At the end of 2022, MDITC became the Ministry of Digital Technologies.

The Ministry of Innovative Development (MID) was established in 2017 and launched the formation and development of the startups ecosystem in the country.[7] Its mission is to implement a unified policy in the field of innovative

---

[7] As a result of a reorganization, MID was subsumed into the newly named Ministry of Higher Education, Science and Innovation as the Agency for Innovation in early 2023.

development to increase the country's intellectual and technological potential. It introduced a procedure for financing startups based on government grants that involve contests.[8] Its tasks have been carried forward by its successor, the Agency for Innovative Development, and include (i) developing and implementing innovations in state building and public development; (ii) introducing innovation in agricultural development, education, and health care; and (iii) improving the regulatory framework for the introduction of innovation and technology.[9]

MID has launched three important programs. First, the Innovative Development and Innovative Ideas Support Fund was set up with an endowment of $5 million. Second, the Center of Technological Excellence was established to conduct incubator and accelerator programs for startups. And third, the Yashnobod Innovative Technological Park was built and provides tax preferences, preferential loans, land, and other opportunities to tenants. During 1988–2022, businesses in the park produced $84 million worth of products and services, of which slightly more than 10% were for export. About 357 jobs were created.

Since the Innovative Development and Innovative Ideas Support Fund is intended to finance the development of science and scientific research, the market has yet to feel the positive impact of this fund on the startup ecosystem.

The government has been particularly active in supporting young entrepreneurs engaged in innovation. Youth technology parks totaling SUM40.8 billion have been established in the Republic of Karakalpakstan and in the regions of Andijan, Samarkand, Syrdarya, Tashkent, and Navoi. About 1,500 young people have participated in scientific and innovative activities in these youth technology parks, and an acceleration program has been launched. There are plans to establish seven more youth technology parks, one each in the regions of Bukhara, Jizzakh, Kashkadarya, Namangan, Fergana, Khorezm, and Surkhandarya.

In 2021, an innovative educational and production technology park, Inno, was built on the student campus of Tashkent (city) on an area of 2 hectares at a cost of SUM114 billion. It is well equipped with facilities, equipment, and supplies and can accommodate about 4,000 young people. Fifty-four prototypes have been developed by young people and 11 startup enterprises have been established, creating 84 jobs.

8   Contests are organized in accordance with Annex 2 of the Resolution of the Cabinet of Ministers No. 133 of 9 March 2020 on the selection and financing of startups.
9   Agency for Innovative Development of the Republic of Uzbekistan.

2.4   New Ways Government Can Support Startups

There are four other ways the government can help build an effective startup ecosystem in Uzbekistan. These are public procurement, better coordination of its units and programs, creating incentives for large companies to link with startups, and training public officials about startups and their needs.

First, procurement is one area where the government could support startups but currently does not. Through its institutions, including schools, hospitals, government agencies, and ministries, the government has enormous spending power. It could be used to collaborate with startups to develop new solutions that increase the efficiency and effectiveness of government operations. More simply, the government can purchase products and services already offered by startups. Currently, government agencies prefer to buy ready-made foreign solutions or develop new solutions internally rather than collaborate with local startups.

New digital innovations could be designed for public administration. Agritech solutions could be adopted by the Ministry of Agriculture and promoted to farmers. Domestic edtech innovations could be adopted in schools, while healthtech solutions could be used in hospitals and clinics. Since there are still many state-owned businesses and banks, they could be encouraged to purchase solutions from startups as part of business-to-business (B2B) activities. Increased procurement of innovations by startups requires modern government procurement policies that incentivize purchases from startups and small businesses. Other countries have introduced such policies.

Second, coordination among government organizations regarding startup development (and the ecosystem) is currently ad hoc and could be improved.[10] Each agency or entity tries to cover all stages of a startup's development, from idea generation to scaling and entering foreign markets. This duplication of effort results in less attention being paid to the specific needs of participants at a particular stage. Although MID should be the main coordinator for ecosystem development, it deals mainly with scientific and biotechnology startups, which are small in number and require a lot of time and support. Developing and adopting a clear strategy where each support program focuses on a specific stage or stages of startup development could be useful. Sector-specific programs would also be helpful to provide focused and tailored advice and support.

Third, the government could also play a greater role in helping large private companies support startups (Box 2). For example, large businesses could be encouraged to establish or support industry-specific incubator and accelerator

---

[10]   UNECE (2022) and UNESCO (2020) also note that coordination in Uzbekistan can be improved.

Box 2: Role of Private Players in Ecosystem Building

A review of experiences in other countries, including Italy, Latvia, Senegal, and Spain, shows that startup laws should aim to involve private players in ecosystem development (Magnetic Latvia n.d. and Ministry of Economic Development 2019).[a] Laws (and policies) can mandate government agencies to provide benefits, preferences, and subsidies to the private sector to encourage its engagement in ecosystem building. These public incentives can encourage the formation of privately run incubators and accelerators and the creation of privately managed coworking spaces and innovation hubs. Incentives can also encourage more high net-worth individuals to come forward as business angels and more corporations and investors to establish private venture capital funds.

By adopting this approach in Uzbekistan, the government could achieve a breakthrough and paradigm shift in startup development.

Source: Authors.

programs. Also, they could provide experienced mentors with sector expertise. Large companies could also establish corporate venture capital funds, as is common in other countries. Finally, large businesses can act as a market for startups' products and services.

Fourth, government officials can be more effective if they have a good understanding of the business community and the needs and challenges of startups. Officials involved with startups could be better trained in this regard, and individuals with private sector experience could be hired to manage programs. In the longer term, experience and capacity need to be built in government support programs.

2.5 Financing

Limited access to finance remains the main obstacle to startup growth in Uzbekistan, according to several studies and the survey conducted for this report (IT Park and TUZ Ventures (n.d.).[11] Currently, several types of funding are available, but most need to be expanded and improved. As noted in Table 3, new types of funding sources may also be added.

In other countries, it is common for startups (and small and medium-sized enterprises) to use bootstrapping to start. Startups in Uzbekistan are similar: they invest their own funds from savings and salaries from regular jobs and solicit funds from family and friends. The average amount ranges from $2,000 to $5,000. This provides the basis for the startup, but additional funds are needed to complete product development and bring it to the market.

---

[11] Uzbekistan Venture Capital Association (in Russian).

Table 3: Sources of Financing by Startup Development Stage

	Seed Stage	Development Stage	Scaling Stage
Source	Own funds, family, friends Government and donor grants Business angels Crowdfunding	VC, angel syndicates, crowdlending, crowdinvesting	VC, bank loans
Examples of providers	Government, donors UzAngels	Government: UzVC, Uzcard VC, Aloqa VC Private: SEMURG VC	International VC: Sturgeon Capital (UK) Battery Road Digital (Singapore)
Number of startups (estimate)	1,000	150	20
Product	Prototyping	Minimum viable product	Product market fit
Characteristics	Ideation	Validation	Expanding market

UK = United Kingdom, VC = venture capital.
Source: Authors.

Banks provide business loans, and the government offers a number of financing programs to channel bank loans to small and medium-sized enterprises on preferential terms. However, the loans must be secured by collateral, which early-stage startups usually cannot provide. Furthermore, the loans need to be serviced (principal repayment and interest), but early-stage startups do not have a revenue stream. Therefore, banks are reluctant to lend to startups, and none of the startups we surveyed received such credit.

Grants are provided by government, donors, and nonprofit organizations and are an important source of funding to supplement bootstrapping. Grants are provided by IT Park Uzbekistan, the United Nations Development Programme, and the Youth Entrepreneurship Support Center.[12] Several startups we interviewed had received grants. However, some grant programs are ad hoc and one-off affairs. In some cases, strict conditions may discourage startups from applying. Therefore, it may be worthwhile to establish more regular grant programs and ensure that the application process is not onerous.

As a startup develops, it will need equity financing from angel investors and venture capital. However, these segments of the financial system remain underdeveloped. In Uzbekistan, there are some angel investors, but their number is limited, and a community of business angels has yet to develop. Other countries have built such a community by offering training courses and tax incentives to potential angel investors and by providing subsidies on investments.[13]

---

[12] IT Park; United Nations Development Programme. Startup Initiatives; Youth Entrepreneurship Support Center of Uzbekistan.

[13] Finland, the Russian Federation, and Israel have undertaken these approaches. See Sk. Reimbursement of Investments to Business Angels (in Russian).

Venture capital is still in its infancy in Uzbekistan. It has not developed organically and is hampered by the lack of a legal framework specifically for private venture capital funds. The government established a fund in 2020 with the creation of the UzVC National Venture Fund by MID. It has investable funds of $1.5 million. As of late 2022, it was not yet operational because the selection of a private management company was still underway. However, the fact that the public funds are managed by a private management company is a good signal for the market. Furthermore, Uzcard, a state-owned payments company, created a corporate venture capital fund of $1 million in 2021. The funds will be allocated to startups in its fintech accelerator. MID has provided financing for startups in all regions (Table 4). Aloqabank has also established a venture capital fund called Aloqaventures in 2021 with an authorized capital of SUM25 billion ($300 million) (UZ Daily 2021). SEMURG VC is a private domestic venture capital fund that has set up. Some foreign funds are active in the country, including Sturgeon Capital from the United Kingdom and Battery Road Digital from Singapore.

Table 4: Funding for Startups by Region, Provided by the Ministry of Innovative Development, 2019–2022

Region	No. of Startups Financed	Amount of Financing (SUM billion)
Tashkent city	46	39.6
Tashkent region	17	14.8
Republic of Karakalpakstan	14	9.4
Fergana	10	6.0
Khorezm	8	6.5
Samarkand	6	6.2
Bukhara	5	1.9
Jizzakh	4	2.7
Andijan	3	1.9
Sirdarya	3	1.1
Surkhandarya	3	1.8
Namangan	2	1.4
Navoi	1	1.0

Source: Government of the Republic of Uzbekistan (direct communication).

On the other hand, the Central Bank's regulation On the Movement of Capital requires a presidential decree or a decision by the Cabinet of Ministers if the amount of funds transferred for an equity investment exceeds $10,000.

In other countries, direct government investment in startups through its own venture capital fund has generally not generated successful results. Officials lack the risk assessment skills to determine which startups or technologies have potential and should be funded. Instead, the government should act as a "funder of funds" by providing capital to (or through) private venture capital funds that are able to assess the risks of startups.[14] It should be noted, however, that the current level of knowledge about startups and ability to assess risk is also limited among investors (angels, venture capital, others). Training is needed to raise this level.

There are three potential financing mechanisms that are not currently used in Uzbekistan. There is no legal or regulatory framework for them. First, crowdfunding is used by startups in other countries to obtain equity investments. Second, convertible loans are also used in other countries, where a startup is first lent funds that are then converted into equity (so that the startup does not have to service a loan). Third, stock option schemes are used for employees of startups in other countries. In such a scheme, an employee's remuneration consists of a salary (cash) and shares (stock) in the company. This reduces a startup's (salary) payments and alleviates the working capital constraints that are often severe in the early stages.

2.6   Incubators and Accelerators

Incubators and accelerators help startups refine their idea, develop a business model, and gain traction in the market. Currently, there are several programs in Uzbekistan. The young age of most startup founders mentioned earlier suggests that startups really need the guidance and practical advice of these programs (and mentors). In addition to limited access to funding, the lack of quality programs is one of the biggest obstacles for startups.

The first initiatives to support and develop the startup ecosystem emerged in 2013–2015. Events and support programs included the Startup Mix Conference, Startup Factory, Startup Accelerator, and others. Most were organized by private organizations such as Brand.uz[15] (currently Tech4impact[16]) together with nongovernment and donor organizations such as the Chamber of Commerce and Industry of Uzbekistan and the United Nations Development Programme.

Over the past 5 years, MID (now AID) has supported 15 accelerator programs and more than 100 workshops, training activities, information sessions, and international meetings. As a result of these initiatives, startup registration for competitions (e.g., pitching, hackathons) have increased many times since 2018, and funding for startups has also increased.

---

[14]   Singapore uses this approach, as does Israel through its Yozma Fund. Indonesia has also moved to this approach.
[15]   Brand.Uz. Conference Startup Mix (in Russian).
[16]   Tech4impact.

Two prominent current programs should be mentioned here. The first is the Youth Entrepreneurship Support Center, established by the nongovernment organization, Youth Union of Uzbekistan, which provides incubation and other activities for startups. The second is a corporate fintech accelerator launched in 2021 by Uzcard, a payment systems company. It is linked to a $1 million corporate venture fund. The accelerator aims to expand Uzcard's network and operations by integrating solutions from local and foreign startups into the Uzcard system, including solutions to automate internal processes. Upon completion of the 6-month acceleration program, startups can qualify for venture capital investments from Uzcard's venture capital fund, whose mandate covers both finance and other business sectors. It is too early to assess the results of the accelerator and its associated fund.

While the current programs are a start, several improvements could be made to make incubators and accelerators more effective. First, there could be more sector-specific programs. Currently, most programs accept startups from all sectors and provide little or no guidance on key sectoral issues or market issues. Second, most programs are unable to provide or connect with high-quality mentors. Furthermore, the available mentors rarely have relevant sector experience for the startups they mentor. The problem is that successful local entrepreneurs are not coming forward to act as mentors. This may be due to a lack of financial incentives, as mentors would like to be paid for their time and advice. It might help if the government or incubators provided funding for such payments. Another option is for startups to "pay" mentors by offering them equity. Third, there are few foreign programs that could bring in higher-level expertise and mentors. Programs for foreigners would provide startups with a broader perspective and encourage them to explore foreign markets in addition to local ones.

2.7 Talent

Capable entrepreneurs and employees are essential to developing viable startups. The founder, in particular, must deal with multiple tasks simultaneously, such as attracting investment, hiring employees, improving technology, designing the business model, and marketing to increase sales. One of the main obstacles for startups in Uzbekistan, according to a recent study, is the lack of educated, skilled, and otherwise qualified employees.[17]

It is a major challenge for startups to find suitable specialists, especially in new technology fields such as big data, blockchain, and artificial intelligence. These specializations are not yet available at universities due to a lack of qualified

---

[17] The results are from the Startup Indicators Uzbekistan 2020 study and can be found at Uzbekistan Venture Capital Association (in Russian).

teachers to produce graduates in these fields. According to one source, there was a 76% increase in job vacancies in the IT sector in January–November in 2020, compared to the same period last year.[18]

Universities are an important source of talent. There are currently 117 universities in the country, including 21 branches of foreign universities and 20 private universities. In 2017, about 9% of secondary school graduates were admitted to universities, but this number was expected to increase to 20% by 2020 due to expanded admissions (Gazeta.uz 2020).

The government is carrying out reforms in the education sector and encouraging the opening of private schools and universities. However, not all of them are helping to produce the talent needed for the startup sector. For example, only one private university specializing in entrepreneurial skills has opened in recent years (TEAM University). To meet the demands of the market, there is a need to provide more and better entrepreneurship skills training.

Some universities, including Westminster International University, Tashkent State University of Economics, and TEAM University, have recently established business incubators. However, due to the lack of suitable faculty and mentors, startups enrolled in these programs acquire few practical business skills. Introducing "Startup as a Diploma" programs at local universities involving foreign experts could more actively engage and train young people in technological entrepreneurship. This approach is currently being tested in India.[19]

---

[18] Spot. 2020. How the Labor Market of IT-Specialists in Uzbekistan Has Changed: Salaries, Supply and Demand (in Russian).

[19] See, for example, India Education Diary (2020).

Ecosystem for Healthtech, Agritech, Edtech, and Cleantech

3

3.1   Survey of Startups

For this study, a survey was conducted among 31 startups in the healthtech, agritech, edtech, and cleantech sectors. Participants were sent a questionnaire followed by an in-depth interview. The survey and interviews covered a range of topics, including characteristics of founders, technology, business models, financing, and factors that hinder the development of startups.

Characteristics of Startups and Their Founders

Most of the startups interviewed were based in Tashkent (22), followed by 3 in Bukhara, 2 in Andijan, and 1 each in Fergana, Karshi, Khorezm, and Namangan. Most of the startups (22) were formed relatively recently, in 2019 or later.

The majority of startups were founded by men (23). The eight startups founded by women were mainly from the health and biotech sectors. Only two of the respondents did not have a university degree (Table 5). Three of the eight women founders have a PhD. The average age of the founders is 31.

Table 5: Summary Statistics of Surveyed Startups

Type of Startup	Number of Startups	Gender Balance		Higher Education		Median Age	
		Female	Male	Female	Male	Female	Male
Healthtech	14	42%	58%	84%	100%	32	31
Agritech	7	22%	78%	100%	86%	38	33.5
Edtech (and e-commerce)	7	0%	100%	n/a	100%	n/a	28
Cleantech	3	33%	66%	100%	100%	38	30.5

n/a = not available.
Source: Authors' survey.

Nearly 90% of the founders had prior experience in their startup's sector. Fourteen of the respondents had previous experience starting a business, and all but one of those had a positive experience. Half of the female founders had a negative experience working in the sector, while the others had either a positive experience (33%) or no experience (17%).

Only five respondents said that their current startup was their only source of income. Half of the respondents were employed elsewhere, and the others ran other businesses (traditional or startups).

Almost half of the startups surveyed are in healthtech, followed by agritech and edtech (Table 6).

Table 6: Sectors of Surveyed Startups

Type of Startup	Number
Healthtech	14
Agritech	7
Cleantech	3
Edtech	7

Notes: One edtech startup can also be classified as e-commerce; two biotech startups were assigned to healthtech and agritech, respectively.
Source: Authors' survey.

Information Technology

All but five of the startups surveyed have a strong digital component, focusing on areas such as big data, artificial intelligence, virtual/augmented reality, and payment systems. One startup focused on blockchain technologies (Table 7).

Table 7: Digital Technologies of Startups

Focus	Technology	Number
Digital technology	Big data	3
	Artificial intelligence	2
	Virtual/augmented reality	2
	Payment systems	1
	Other	19
Non-IT		5

IT = information technology.
Source: Authors' survey results.

3.2 Healthtech Startups

Healthtech is an emerging field, but it is still at an early stage of development in Uzbekistan. Many healthtech startups have already been established and also make up the majority of the startups surveyed for this study (Table 8). Many are in the product development stage, and few have stable revenue streams.

There is considerable opportunity in this area. COVID-19 has created a high demand for healthtech products and telemedicine services to overcome lockdown measures and social distancing requirements. Even after the end of movement restrictions, the use of internet-based services is likely to become part of the new normal.

In addition, the government is paying close attention to the digitalization of this sector and is allocating considerable resources to it. The National Chamber of Innovative Healthcare was established by the Ministry of Health in 2019. Its three main tasks are (i) to develop a strategy and proposals for an innovative model of health-care management; (ii) to digitalize and otherwise improve the collection and analysis of medical statistics; and (iii) to create a system for registering doctors and pharmacists

Table 8: Healthtech Startups

Startup	Project Description
VR-Cerebri	Rehabilitation technique for people with Parkinson's disease using virtual reality glasses
StomaCRM	Helps dentists and clinic owners automate work processes and reduce paperwork to save time and reduce costs
DryPants	Device that detects the level of wetness in a diaper and help parents potty train infants
TumorOnTarget	Method to determine the status of tumor marker HER2 based on a polymerase chain reaction (PCR) test
Vegan Uz	Produces and delivers vegan meals for people who want to improve their diet, lose weight, and/or follow dietary restrictions
Porous insole	Specialized footwear for patients with diabetes mellitus to prevent gangrene of the legs and reduce the risk of disability (based on physiological and biomechanical properties of diabetic foot pathology)
Mammo Cancer AI	Breast cancer diagnosis using artificial intelligence
WoundCareLab	Innovative dressing for wounds of varying complexity
Mdoktor	Mobile application to provide interactive health-care services to the public
Tashxisuz	Portal that connects patients with doctors (to save time and cost), allows patients to self-diagnose with up to 80% accuracy, and contact an appropriate doctor online
Dental Gel	Gel to prevent diseases of the hard tissues of the teeth and oral mucosa in children with congenital cleft lip and palate
MyRP	Transmits prescriptions from the doctor to the patient and from the patient to the pharmacy (or doctor direct to pharmacy) through an electronic prescription exchange network
Smart Medical and MedData	Automated enterprise resource planning systems for medical and health clinics

Source: Authors.

and providing a single, publicly accessible electronic database. With interesting ideas, healthtech startups can play an important role by offering their innovations to help achieve these goals. However, for this to happen, the government needs to be more open to procuring and adopting innovations from startups.

One problem with the current approach of startups in Uzbekistan is that they rely on innovations from abroad and merely try to adapt them to local conditions. Thus, there are hardly any real innovations, which should be the focus of tech startups' activities.

Characteristics of Founders

The founders of the 14 startups surveyed in the healthtech sector tended to be young, relatively well-educated, and experienced in working for or running a startup.[20] There was also a high proportion of women. Most of the founders were not involved in their healthtech startup full-time, but had salaried jobs, were running other companies at the same time, or were still in education.

The average age of the founders is 31. The vast majority (85%) have startup experience. With women accounting for 42% of the founders surveyed, women are more strongly represented in healthtech than in other sectors. This sector accounts for 75% of all female founders among the 30 startups surveyed across the four sectors. This reflects the proportion of women in higher education in health care in Uzbekistan, the only area of study with more than 50% women.

Eight founders reported having studied in the field of their startup, while seven (one woman and six men) had completed higher education. Three founders have a PhD, and they are all women. Three male respondents have a degree in IT, while two (one female and one male) have a degree in business/finance.

Only three of the founders work exclusively for their startup. Seven founders combine the development of their startup with paid employment elsewhere. Others run a separate business or are still completing their education. Half of the founders have previously operated a startup and had positive experiences.

Nature of the Startups

The startups surveyed in this sector tend to be recently established, small, and generate little or no revenue. Most have more than one founder, and most are engaged in adapting innovations from other countries.

---

[20] Many startups have cofounders or joint founders. The characteristics described in this section each refer to one of the founders of a startup.

All 14 startups were established between 2019 and 2021. Many were founded in response to increased demand for medical services and the trend toward decentralized medical services triggered by the COVID-19 pandemic. All but two of the startups employed fewer than six people. Only about one-third of the startups had a single founder. All 14 startups had only founders as owners of their companies and no outside investors. Of the respondents, 50% reported working from home, but also occasionally use university campuses and laboratories. The remainder is almost evenly split between those who use coworking spaces and those who work in rented space.

Innovation, Models, and Markets

Most of the startups said their product idea came from an existing product abroad. The other four startups developed truly unique innovations. However, about two-thirds of the 14 startups conduct their own market research, while others rely on existing sources. Half of the startups test their solutions based on customer feedback, while others use focus groups.

The vast majority of startups said their business model focused on direct sales. Subscriptions and ads were other expected sources of income. About three-quarters of the startups expect to sell to other businesses, the so-called business-to-business (B2B) model. Other target groups included government agencies and consumers, with some startups targeting more than one type of client. Most startups focused on the domestic market. Half said their products were designed for the domestic market, while the others said they did not have the funds to export or that they would start with the domestic market and then decide whether to try to export. With almost all of the startups in the formative stages and focused on product development, only one of the startups had established a distribution channel.

Finance

Securing funding is a major challenge for the health-care startups surveyed. Access to funding is currently very limited, in part because these startups are small, young, and in most cases still in the project development stage with little market engagement. Of the 14 startups surveyed, 12 had not generated any revenue in the past 12 months, and none had received external funding from a venture capital fund or business angel. Three had received a government grant, one had obtained a loan, and the rest had so far relied solely on their own savings and contributions from family and friends.

When asked about their current focus, 11 of the 14 startups said they were focused on fundraising. And for future growth, 13 said they need venture funding. Only two had applied for venture capital, one of which had been rejected and the other was still awaiting a decision at the time of the survey. Only two startups had applied for a loan, one of which was approved for SUM20 million. As with startups in other countries, loan financing is probably not a viable option, as it often requires collateral (which these small startups do not have) and a revenue stream to service the loan, which is also lacking in the early stages.

Given the early stage of these enterprises, most indicated that they spent the funds available to them on product development. Salaries were also an important expense.

A small number of startups (2) wanted investor funding only. Seventy-eight percent wanted assistance in solving business problems that arose, and half expected investors to help them find the right contacts in the business community (Table 9). A total of 42% wanted assistance in approaching new clients. Several respondents wanted investors to provide multiple types of support. The desire for nonfinancial assistance from investors could indicate that founders do not know how to manage a business and build a network. It could also indicate that this type of nonfinancial support and guidance is not being provided by other players who should be providing it, such as incubators, accelerators, and mentors.

Table 9: Healthtech Startups' Desired Assistance from Investors

Type of Assistance Sought from Investor	Share of Healthtech Startups Surveyed (%)
Solving arising issues	78
Finding right connections	50
Reaching new clients	42
Supporting strategy development	21
Finding new investors	7

Source: Authors' survey.

Acceleration Programs and Government Support

Most startups (12 of 14 surveyed) had participated in government acceleration programs. Slightly more than half found the program useful for product development and finalization. As a result of the acceleration program, some firms were able to obtain grant funding. Other benefits included assistance in conducting market research, skills development (in business planning), and guidance in managing teams.

Two-thirds of startups said there were no legal or regulatory barriers constraining their operations. However, three cited a lack of regulations in the health sector, and two cited tax regulations as a barrier. When asked more generally what startups need for future growth, only one startup cited government support.

In general, startups said they wanted support in building networks and connections with businesses, customers, and other players in the ecosystem.

Talent

Some startups have difficulty recruiting qualified personnel for their operations. Half of the startups said they have problems hiring developers, and another three find it difficult to recruit employees with skills relevant to their products. On the other hand, three of the 14 startups said they have no problems recruiting the right people. In addition, a quarter of the startups had problems with high staff turnover.

3.3 Agritech Startups

Agriculture is an important industry in Uzbekistan, accounting for 23% of gross domestic product and employing half of the population. In this regard, startups are somewhat more established than in other sectors and may have better prospects for sustainability (Table 10). Given the specific nature of agricultural activities, which are different in each country, digital solutions need to be adapted to pave the way for more startups in the digital space.

There are high barriers for international technological solutions to enter the market. In addition, agricultural conditions vary from country to country. These two factors provide an opportunity for local startups. In fact, most startups have adopted ideas from abroad to develop their product or service. Another supporting factor is that the government is prioritizing the digitalization of the agriculture sector.

Table 10: Agritech Startups

Startup	Innovation
Defuse It	Water purification equipment for irrigation, with an intelligent control system
Gardens of Babylon	Vertical phyto-farm using artificial intelligence and blockchain to cultivate agricultural products and aromatic and medicinal plants in difficult climatic and urban conditions
Aziz Nigmatov	Automated monitoring system to assess the current state of groundwater
Agromart.uz	Digital platform offering digital services to farmers and other stakeholders
Trator	Mobile phone application for farm-to-farm exchange of agricultural machinery
Life Map	Processes the agro-market throughout the country and provides tools on a geo-information platform to increase the efficiency of agriculture and the use of water resources
UZGPS-AGRO	Monitoring and control system for the operation of agricultural machinery that increases the efficiency of use

Source: Authors.

Startup Founders

Seven agritech startups were surveyed. The average age of the founders was 34. Only one founder was female. All but one had completed higher education, four in IT or a technical field and the others in education and business. None of the founders focused exclusively on their startup. Three combined the development of their startup with employment elsewhere, while three launched other startups in parallel. One founder ran another business. Three had previous experience with their own startups, while the other four were newcomers to creating a startup (but already had experience with startups). All but one of the startups had more than one founder. None had external shareholders or owners. All were based in Tashkent, which may be somewhat surprising given that agriculture is a rural activity.

Innovation, Markets, and Business Models

In five of the seven cases, the product idea came from existing products from abroad, while the other two were unique innovations. All but one of the startups surveyed stated that their products were unique to the Uzbek market.

Furthermore, four of the startups conducted their own market research. In terms of testing, four startups tested their products through customer feedback, while one startup each used focus groups, laboratory testing, and complex research testing.

In terms of clientele, four of the seven startups sell to other businesses (B2B) and three of them sell to government agencies (B2G). One startup sells directly to consumers (B2C) and there is also a complex B2B2C model. So, in total, there are nine models used by seven startups, with two enterprises using more than one model.

The three B2G startups can be explained by the fact that the government continues to play an important role in the sector and is therefore an important client for agritech firms. Farmers are not allowed to own their own land but lease it from the government. Local governments decide what to grow (mostly cotton and wheat) and how much can be grown. Seeds, fertilizer, oil, and other inputs are then provided centrally. The harvesting process is also centralized. Startups are trying to enter different areas of the market. Still, startups face the challenge of finding the right connections to market their products and services.

There are various players such as the Farmers' Union and the Ministry of Agriculture that are trying to promote digital transformation in the sector. The government's Digital Uzbekistan 2030 strategy does contain actions related to agriculture and the promotion of smart farms.[21] In addition, the Galla information system is being

---

[21] See Digital Uzbekistan 2030.

commissioned to monitor the harvest of cotton and wheat. However, besides these, there is so far no evidence that efficient digital products are being widely used or promoted by government players. The Farmers' Union and other associations do not have the capacity to play a facilitating role. Therefore, the establishment of a center in the form of a public–private partnership (such as AgTech Garage in Brazil) that could act as a facilitator and digital hub between agritech startups and stakeholders should be considered.

Finance

Agritech startups are more operational than those in healthtech. More than half of them have a revenue stream, although in some cases it is still small. Lack of funding was cited by 57% as their main problem.

One of the startups surveyed, Gardens of Babylon, has received external investment of up to $100,000. None of the startups have received or applied for venture capital or a bank loan. Most startups are not adequately informed about venture capital funding opportunities. Most relied on their founders' capital supplemented by international or government grants. One company, Defuse It, was funded by a university. Funds were spent mainly on product development, followed by salaries. Meanwhile, nearly half of the respondents hoped to raise new funding, with targeted amounts ranging from less than $100,000 to more than $1 million.

Three startups said they expected nothing more than funding from potential investors. The other four sought advice on business issues, new connections, access to new clients, and strategy development (Table 11).

Table 11: Agritech Startups' Desired Assistance from Investors

Nonfinancial Support Desired from Investors	Share of Enterprises Surveyed (%)
None	43
Solving arising issues	29
Finding right connections	43
Reaching out to new clients	29
Supporting development of strategy	4

Source: Authors' survey.

Acceleration Programs and Government Support

Four of the seven startups participated in government acceleration programs. Two benefited in product development and completion, one in raising funds, and the other in project redesign and launch.

Regarding further development of their startups, 71% said they needed venture capital for further growth, 57% added they needed better networks and connections, 14% said they needed access to knowledge, and 14% needed a business partner.

In addition, 86% of startups said there were no legal barriers to their business, while 14% cited tax regulations as a barrier. When asked about export potential, two of the startups said their products were designed for local use, one said they wanted to test them locally, and four said they had no resources for export.

Government institutions do not tend to support local startups. Instead, they develop their own solutions with the support of international organizations, which have not proven effective.

Internet Coverage and Digitalization

In remote areas where most agricultural producers are located, internet access is still sparse, making it difficult to reach them with digital services and to use digital applications at the field level. Startups expressed a general concern that the government lacks a coordinated approach to digitalization. There is no clear division of which ministry or agency is responsible for which aspects of the digitalization process.

Talent

Only two of the seven startups had problems hiring qualified personnel, notably developers, but also people with product knowledge. Only one startup had a high staff turnover.

3.4 Edtech Startups

The education sector is on the rise in Uzbekistan in the wake of major reforms and liberalization. Considering the very young age of the population (25 years), this sector offers interesting opportunities for the use of digital technologies. In addition, the COVID-19 pandemic and subsequent lockdowns have led to high demand for distance learning resources. In response, the government has rapidly expanded access to remote learning options.

In addition to schools, universities and other tertiary institutions have begun to digitize their program offerings and management systems. They have turned to foreign solutions, but these may not be adaptable to the Uzbek environment. In this context, there are great opportunities for edtech startups to provide locally adapted solutions for all levels of education. However, it is important that government authorities (ministries of education) and institutions are open to using local edtech solutions. In 2018, the Center for Innovations, Technologies and Strategies was established in the Ministry of Public Education to introduce modern innovative technologies in the education system and conduct strategic analysis in this regard.

Characteristics of Founders

Most of the seven startups had multiple founders, but only male founders participated in the survey (Table 12). In terms of education, all of the founders surveyed had higher education, with just under half of them in IT and the others in business, finance, and non-IT technical fields.

Table 12: Edtech Startups

Startup	Innovation
MaktRon Interactive	Training system that uses machine learning to track progress and provide online competition
Scratch	Educational manual on programming, for teachers
Roboteach	Application that enables distance learning in Uzbek and English, with all video tutorials and tests loaded into the app
Eduportal 2.0	Platform with 120,000 books and audiobooks from the Ziyonet network and literature from the Eduportal network, which develops video tutorials and tests for each subject taught in school
Int42H	Platform for massive open online courses using artificial intelligence and blockchain technology
Prep.uz	Platform where teachers post their teaching materials and set the cost of providing courses
Coozin.uz	Platform where households can sell homemade food online, with a focus on training future chefs (to empower women)

Source: Authors.

The founders of edtech startups are the youngest of all the sectors surveyed and are between 26 and 30 years old. Some of them had previous experience with startups. One founder reported a positive experience with a previous startup, while another reported a negative experience. In only one case was there a sole founder. In addition, only one founder focused exclusively on his startup (Coozin.uz), while the others combined the development of their startup with other employment or managing another business. For example, one founder gave lectures as a source of income. Only one company, MaktRon Interactive, had an equity shareholder (business angel) who was not one of the founders.

Just under half of the startups surveyed were founded before 2019. Five of the seven startups employed 10 people or fewer. The others employed no more than 30 people. Most used rented office space, and one worked from home.

Compared with the three other sectors surveyed, edtech startups are the most geographically dispersed. Four are based in Tashkent and one each in Bukhara, Fergana, and Karshi.[22]

Business Models

Three-quarters of the startups surveyed offer services on a subscription basis. Other modes include direct sales, online sales, transaction-based sales, and in one case, a freemium. Several startups combined more than one sales model. In terms of clients, all but one sold to consumers (B2C), and many had multiple types of clients (including B2B and B2G). Two startups were in the growth stage, while three were in the seed stage and two were on pause and thus not operating.

One startup has a globally unique product, while four indicated that their products are somewhat unique to the Uzbek market. One startup has developed an improved technology for the local market, while the other uses an existing technology. Only one startup has exported its product, and the others seemed to have little interest in doing so. Three-quarters conducted their own market research, while the others relied on existing sources. Most startups rely on customer feedback to test their products, while two startups use focus groups.

Finance

Five of the seven startups are not yet generating any revenue or are generating little revenue. The other two generate less than $100,000 annually.

Only one startup received external investment (up to $100,000) provided by a business angel (MaktRon Interactive). The same startup applied for venture capital but was unable to reach an agreement with the fund on the valuation of the company. The other startups relied on their own funds and government grants, with one startup receiving a foreign grant. None of the startups received or applied for a loan. All startups indicated that most of the funds were used for product development. All startups indicated that they needed access to venture capital for future growth. Three startups planned to raise funding, with the targeted amount ranging up to $500,000.

---

22 Some edtech startups have an e-commerce component.

Most of the startups surveyed hoped that an investor would provide more than just funding (Table 13). More than half of the respondents wanted assistance in reaching out to new clients, solving problems that arise, and making good connections. Support in strategy development was also desired.

Table 13: Edtech Startups' Desired Assistance from Investors

Nonfinancial Support Desired from Investors	Share of Enterprises Surveyed (%)
Reaching out to new clients	85
Solving arising issues	72
Finding the right connections	57
Support for strategy development	42
Operational management	14

Source: Authors' survey.

Acceleration Programs

About three-quarters of the startups surveyed had participated in a government acceleration program (and one in an international program). The programs were helpful for product development and finalization, and for obtaining funding (government grants).

Other Challenges and Obstacles

The majority of startups said they needed to develop better networking and connections, while two others needed access to knowledge, and one faced the challenge of scaling up to access other markets.

Four startups said they were having problems hiring qualified personnel, especially developers and product-related specialists. Two startups said they were not looking for new staff, but three had high staff turnover.

Four startups said there were too many bureaucratic regulations, and two of them had difficulty registering educational licenses. The other three startups said they had not encountered legal or regulatory obstacles.

3.5   Cleantech Startups

In agriculture, the policy of centrally planned intensive farming has left little room for sustainable solutions. Awareness of the impact of agriculture on the environment has only recently been explored in Uzbekistan. Therefore, in the next decade, this will be a fast-growing market where competitive local cleantech solutions can be developed. Sustainable agriculture is in vogue and will play a larger role in Uzbekistan's agricultural policy in the near future.

In the energy sector, private companies are allowed to sell energy, but there is no working mechanism, so there are no players in the market yet. This could change with the introduction of large renewable energy players (such as Masdar and Total), which could present an opportunity for cleantech startups in the services and B2C solutions. Multilateral and bilateral development partners can play a role in helping local cleantech startups test solutions.

In 2019, the laws on Use of Renewable Energy Sources and on Public-Private Partnership were passed, providing a regulatory framework for the implementation of renewable energy projects. These laws provide benefits and preferences for renewable energy producers. However, the implementation mechanisms to support cleantech have yet to be developed.

Another advantage of the Uzbek market is the system of scientific institutions that could play a role in testing new technologies and solutions without high investments.

Characteristics of Founders

Three startups were surveyed in this sector (Table 14). One of them was led by a woman. All three founders have a degree in agriculture and two have studied in the area where they started their company. The average age of the founders is 33. Only one has experience starting a business. One startup was founded before 2019, the others after. One of the startups has a sole founder, the other two have multiple founders. One of the three companies has attracted an outside investor as

Table 14: Cleantech Startups

Startup	Innovation
Compost.uz	A technology innovation for Uzbekistan that transforms residues and agricultural waste into organic fertilizer
Bio Innocens	Biological products to reduce plant pests and diseases
Adjacent Power	Green technology to promote the use of renewable energy at affordable prices

Source: Authors.

a business angel and current co-owner. One founder focuses entirely on the startup (sole source of income), while the others combine their startup work with either employment or running another business. All three are based in Tashkent.

All three startups are registered as businesses and employ 10 people or fewer. Two of them have rented office space, while the other owns its own office space. Two reported annual revenues between $10,000 and $100,000, while the other startup has no revenues.

Startup Idea and Business Model

Two founders indicated that the idea for the startup came from an existing product abroad, while the other has a completely new product for which there is no equivalent elsewhere. Two companies conducted their own research for baseline data, while the other used existing data sources. Two companies conduct tests based on customer feedback, while the other conducts tests in a lab. None of the startups export.

All three startups use a direct sales business model, while one also offers subscriptions. All sold to other businesses (B2B) and one also sold to government agencies (B2G). All said their products were unique to the Uzbek market and based on technologies available worldwide.

Each of the three startups is at a different stage of development: seed, growth, and scaling. The startups' current activities are focused on sales, fundraising, and capitalization.

Finances

One startup received an external investment of up to $100,000 from a business angel. None of the startups obtained a loan, although one application was denied. All have investments (savings) from their founders, and one received an international grant. Two startups indicated that most of the funding was spent on product development, while the other mentioned team composition. Two cited lack of funding as the main problem, and all said they needed venture capital to grow and would use the funds for product improvements. Only one startup had applied for (foreign) venture capital funding. The application was rejected because the fund did not invest in cleantech.

Two startups indicated that they expected funding only from potential investors, while the other startup wanted assistance in solving problems, making new connections, and reaching new clients. Only one startup participated in an acceleration program that was helpful in raising funds.

Talent and Regulations

One of the three startups said it had problems hiring qualified employees, especially those with product-related knowledge. Two indicated that they do not have high staff turnover. Two startups cited lack of regulations in their respective fields as a barrier, while the other had not encountered any legal or regulatory barriers.

Industry Challenges

There is concern that the government does not yet actively support clean technologies and that in agriculture the chemical (fertilizer) industry lobby continues to exert a strong influence on policy. Furthermore, the government dominates the energy sector, and cooperation with private players is limited. Public–private partnerships (e.g., power purchase agreements) are not used. In addition, the government could stimulate startups by acting as a customer (i.e., procurement), but it has not done so to date.

The industry typically consists of hard components (i.e., not apps or web platforms) that require specialized skills. As a result, the initial cost of developing a new product and launching it is high. All or most components are manufactured overseas, and there are no customs preferences. On the demand side, awareness of clean technologies is low among stakeholders and consumers in both the agriculture and energy sectors.

Given the nature of these markets and the unfamiliarity of investors, venture capital is reluctant to fund startups, leaving funds scarce.

Recommendations

The government has begun to pay special attention to the development of innovation and technological entrepreneurship. The tech startup ecosystem is emerging, but more efforts are needed to make it fully functional and mature. The following recommendations are made to support these efforts.

Strategy and Coordination

Create and implement a coordinated strategy. Several ministries and agencies are involved in supporting innovative entrepreneurship and startups. These include the Ministry of Higher Education, Science and Innovation; the Ministry for Digital Technologies; the Youth Union of Uzbekistan; the Chamber of Commerce and Industry of Uzbekistan; the IT Park; and others. Their activities are currently running in parallel with little coordination. Therefore, a coordination strategy could be developed and implemented by a new joint body (steering committee, working group, commission, etc.).

Support a life-cycle or development-stage approach to startup support. Incubators and accelerators, as well as support agencies, should take a stage approach in their programs. This means that startups have different needs and face different challenges depending on whether they are in the ideation, pre-seed, seed, growth, scaling, or other stage of their development. The transition from incubation to acceleration is an important step, and startups should be able to move cleanly from one stage to the next. Early-stage support can prepare startups to reach a state that makes them attractive to venture capital.

Create a unified database for the ecosystem. To track and measure the pulse of the ecosystem's development, the government can create a unified database of all startups. This can be used to analyze the development of startups based on a number of metrics. It can also be used by investors to identify and select promising companies for investment.

Provide better support to the regions. The ecosystem is strongest in the capital, Tashkent. Efforts should be made to ensure that support services and finance are available to would-be startup entrepreneurs in the regions to build a balance community of startups.

Finance

Continue and expand grant funding. Grants of $2,000 to $4,000 can provide significant support to startups in the ideation stage, when the innovation is being developed but not yet generating revenue. Grants can be accessed on a competitive basis (e.g., through pitch competitions).

Channel public capital to angel investors and private venture capital. The private sector can assess risk and innovation better than the public sector. Therefore, the government can channel its venture capital to angels and venture capital funds for the latter to invest in startups.

Operationalize the National Venture Fund. The National Venture Fund will be managed by a private company and is expected to operate on a sound commercial basis. Full operationalization of the fund needs to be completed. The personnel working for the fund should be well trained and have experience in private investments. Training can be provided by foreigners who have expertise in fund management and risk-based investing.

Provide tax incentives for private venture capital funds and angel investors. There is a need to encourage more angel investors to come forward and for new venture capital funds to be established. The government can help through tax incentives, such as lower taxation of capital gains from startups or offsetting losses from startups against other tax liabilities.

Provide the legal basis (instruments) to attract investment. Legislation is needed to better protect investors' rights and encourage investment. This could include an appropriate legal framework for convertible loans and clear legal formats for large companies to partner with or invest in (smaller) startups. The legal framework for stock option plans can also be established to allow startups with low revenues to partially compensate their employees by offering company shares.

Talent Development

Develop a skilled workforce for startups. There is a need for greater skills for startups. These include the skills of founders in entrepreneurship, business management, financing, and human resources management. This also includes skilled employees, especially developers/programmers and people with product expertise. Currently, there are programs and courses at universities that teach these skills. These programs can be improved and expanded. Language is also a barrier in many cases. Most founders do not speak English or Russian and therefore face a barrier in acquiring new knowledge and skills from abroad, introducing new foreign technologies, and soliciting investment from outsiders. Language training can be improved in the school system and through other programs.

Offer training for a range of players and needs in the ecosystem. Programs could include (a) training successful entrepreneurs to be good mentors; (b) training potential entrepreneurs how to start a startup; (c) training investors, including high net-worth individuals, how to invest in startups; (d) training incubator program managers and staff how to better run their programs; and (e) teaching business English. Furthermore, universities may introduce "startup-as-a-diploma" programs, where students can submit their startup business plan instead of an academic paper or master's thesis to fulfill university requirements. In many cases, the good trainers and experts can be hired from abroad to provide their expertise in Uzbekistan.

Strengthen digital literacy. Digital skills are weak or nonexistent in parts of the population. This reduces the market (client base) for startups whose innovations are digitally based.

Foreign Expertise

Improve the quality of startup support by engaging foreign experts, mentors, and programs. Domestic startup development programs are generally of lower quality than foreign programs. Therefore, current programs (such as incubators and accelerators) should seek to engage foreign experts and match startups with foreign mentors where possible. In addition, branches of foreign incubator and accelerator programs should be encouraged to set up in Uzbekistan or be engaged to provide advice to local programs.

Procurement

Encourage public procurement from startups. Ministries, agencies, and other public entities need to increase procurement of innovations from startups. This includes edtech solutions for schools; healthtech solutions for clinics and hospitals; and cleantech solutions for energy, pollution and industrial water, and waste. Procurement policies and procedures could be revised to ensure that startups have the same opportunities as large suppliers. State-owned enterprises could learn how to work with startups and how to incorporate their solutions into their processes and infrastructure.

Startup Communities

Encourage startup associations and communities. There are few platforms, communities, or associations that bring startups together to share experiences and support each other. These could be encouraged. In other countries, there are sector-specific associations, such as a fintech or a healthtech association.

Appendix

Digital Uzbekistan

The development of the digital economy is assessed by various indicators, including the share of the digital economy in the gross domestic product (GDP), the size of investments in information and communication technology (ICT), the speed of the internet, its coverage of the country's territory and its availability for use by the population, the level of development of e-commerce, the share of public services in the e-government system, the sufficient number of ICT specialists in organizations, etc.

In 2016–2020, the volume of services provided by the information and communication industry doubled from SUM6.3 trillion to SUM12.9 trillion and accounted for 1.5% of GDP. The length of fiber-optic communication lines increased almost 3.8 times from 17,900 to 68,600 kilometers (km). The number of base stations for mobile communications increased by 1.8 times from 17,700 to 31,700 units, and more than 5,600 new mobile stations were installed and put into operation nationwide in 2020 alone. The number of mobile subscribers has increased by 20% since 2016 to 25.4 million people, and the number of internet users has almost doubled to 22.5 million people, representing 66% of the population.

To date, all kindergartens, medical institutions, and more than 8,000 schools have access to high-speed internet. The increase in the number of mobile and internet users has been fueled not only by the development of ICT infrastructure, but also by a decrease in the cost of internet use while increasing speed. Since 2016, the bandwidth (speed) of the international data transfer network has increased by almost 22 times—from 55 to 1,200 gigabytes per second. At the same time, the cost of internet providers' tariffs has fallen from $91.50 to $4.30 per megabit per second.

In October 2020, the Digital Uzbekistan 2030 strategy was approved, which envisages the implementation of more than 280 projects for the digital transformation of regions and sectors over the next 2 years. It aims to double the share of digital services in GDP by 2025 by allocating about $2.5 billion for the development of digital infrastructure.

According to the strategy, by 2030, it is envisaged to

1. increase the number of startups enrolled in the incubation and acceleration programs of technology parks from the current 50 to 2,500 per year;
2. increase the number of higher and secondary educational institutions for training IT specialists from the current 7,000 to 20,000;
3. increase the country's high-speed internet coverage from 67% to 100% by increasing the length of fiber-optic cables from 41,000 km to 250,000 km;
4. increase the share of providing high-speed internet to social institutions such as educational and medical institutions from 45% to 100% by 2022;
5. increase the proportion of e-government services provided through the single interactive portal[1] of public services from 34% to 90%; and
6. increase the number of internet banking users from the current 10 million to 20 million.

The strategy also envisages the expansion of digitalization in the health-care sector and the completion of the implementation of the electronic polyclinic and telemedicine systems in the regions. The digital transformation of the banking sector will continue, including automated management systems and financial technologies. For the digitalization of agriculture, it is planned to attract more than $600 million for the introduction of modern agricultural technologies and innovative solutions from abroad.

No less important is Uzbekistan's place in international rankings that assess the level of development of information technologies and technological entrepreneurship.

Uzbekistan has achieved positive results in 2016–2020:

1. According to the ICT Development Index, Uzbekistan improved its rank from 103 to 95 among 176 countries, with an index of 4.9.
2. According to the E-Government Development Index, which is compiled on the basis of three indicators—development of online public services, telecommunications infrastructure, and human capital development— Uzbekistan ranks 87th among 193 countries. Currently, the number of public services provided by the Single Interactive Public Services portal has reached 300 in 20 areas of public services.

However, it should be noted that Uzbekistan does not yet appear in a number of other indices, such as the World Economic Forum, the Global Competitiveness Index, or the GEM score.

---

[1] The Single portal was created in order to provide users with access to electronic public services. See About a Single Portal.

References

Durban, J. 2021. What's the Difference between a Startup, a Scale-up, and a Tech Company?. Early Metrics.

Gazeta.uz. 2020. Ministry of Higher Education – About Plans in the Field of Higher Education (in Russian). Tashkent.

Government of Uzbekistan. 2017. *Decree of the President. About the Action Strategy for the Further Development of the Republic of Uzbekistan*. No. UP-4947. 7 February. Tashkent.

Government of Uzbekistan. 2018. *Decree of the President. On Additional Measures to Improve the Mechanisms for Financing Projects in the Field of Entrepreneurship and Innovation*. No. UP-5583. 24 November. Tashkent.

Government of Uzbekistan. 2019. *Resolution of the Cabinet of Ministers. On Approval of the Regulation on the Activity of Investment and Management Companies*. No. 414. 17 May. Tashkent.

Government of Uzbekistan. 2020. *Law of the Republic of Uzbekistan on Innovative Activity*. No. LRU-630. 19 June. Tashkent.

India Education Diary. 2020. Startup as a Diploma.

IT Park and TUZ Ventures. n.d. Report on the Startup Market of Uzbekistan. Tashkent.

Magnetic Latvia. n.d. Startup Law. Presentation slides.

Ministry of Economic Development. 2019. The Italian Startup Act. Presentation slides. Tashkent.

StartupGrind. n.d. 5 Lessons from Age versus Startup Success in India (Data Driven). Blog. Palo Alto.

United Nations Commission for Europe (UNECE). 2022. *Innovation for Sustainable Development: Review of Uzbekistan*. Geneva.

United National Educational, Scientific and Cultural Organization (UNESCO). 2020. *Mapping Research and Innovation in the Republic of Uzbekistan*. Paris.

UZ Daily. 2021. Aloqabank Establishes a Venture Fund Aloqaventure. Tashkent.

www.ingramcontent.com/pod-product-compliance
Lightning Source LLC
Chambersburg PA
CBHW042035220326
41599CB00045BA/7428